SIGNAL to NOISE

SIGNAL
to NOISE
Eve Luckring

ORNITHOPTER PRESS   CHEVY CHASE

First Edition

Published by Ornithopter Press
www.ornithopterpress.com

ISBN 978-1-942723-20-2

Library of Congress Control Number: 2025938657

Cover image:
Impression Figure, c. 1885-1904
pigment on glass
by Margaret Watts Hughes

Design and composition by Mark Harris

in memory of Elizabeth and Viola

…into the dark river with its wrist, its thirst.
Its lust, its list, its amethyst.

—Joyelle McSweeney

1.

It's the far end of twilight and I struggle to see where I am in the low blue shadowy—the tide coming in; most of the beach swallowed; the air, damp cold. My belongings are scattered; a balled-up towel and a half-buried handbag, its contents strewn about. Poking up out of mounded sand, I see the top corner of my driver's license. I pick it up, relieved to find it intact; its face looking blankly into the blank between us. Other possessions have suffered various sorts of violations: ripped, cracked, broken into pieces; I am dispersed.

A raven, I think. A comforting thought compared to the other things I think. The surf approaches fast and rough at my back. The sky, heavy. Where are my sandals? The wind, gritty, stinging, pushes me forcefully toward a dark thick of trees ahead when I suddenly remember the warm clear calm I dozed off in. Careless of me to forget how fast the weather can change.

I hear a voice calling my name;
I can't tell from which direction or how close it might be.

I can't tell if it wants to harm me or tell me something
important; I know it wants attention.

"Say the word 'Haint'…"
"Say the word 'Strop'…"
"Say the word 'Rift'…"
"Say the word 'Lure'…"
"Say the word 'Whom'…"

A rhythm pulses through the center of my body. Repeats. Repeats again. It's familiar, but I can't quite place where I know it from… With the next reprise the cadence travels through the tip of my tongue…Ah, I realize…it's a sound— a sound I cannot hear. I recognize the vibrations like the footsteps of a dear friend, overjoyed to be in their presence again. I open the window and turn my better ear to the early December sunset. Low clouds muffle the dusk. Hoohooohooooooo hoo hoo, Hoohooo hooooooo who hoo, Hoohooohooooooo who whoo

Some said the cause was diabolical; some said it was unidentifiable.

Words began to shape-shift because the syllables got their hearing confused. A few kept cover and eventually ran away, pitched far afield.

Some said the cause was biological; some said it was unverifiable.

Crowds and cars ran over the tell.

Then the owls vanished, along with parts of your voice.

You say the word "fog;" I hear "sob."
You say "which;" I hear "with."
You say "needs;" I hear "means."
A fog which needs... a sob with means...

I hear a voice calling her name.
I can't tell how far away she is or from which side she answers.

I can't tell if she knows I am listening.
I hear her crying.

She gestures to me, seated in the first row of a small audience assembled in folding chairs, introducing me as the author of what she begins to read:

"I received a love letter today…"

Her voice is mellifluous. I know she is speaking in language, but all I hear is tone, a spell cast over every syllable, each phrase beside itself, pleading. The words weep. My body involuntarily starts to sway back and forth, back and forth, back and forth…

Abruptly, the audience chuckles. I'm confused, though I can't seem to care. The reader's undulating voice lures me into an ever-expanding lemniscate of anguish, back and forth, back and forth…I empty, crack open, entirely bereft when the audience laughs again, louder, longer; the bright staccato of their amusement reverberating an incomprehensible chasm between us.

On opposite sides of its echo, we listen, possessed by diametrical energies—they, the entertained audience, and I, a snake charmed out of its basket, ready to meet what holds the air just beyond striking distance.

"Say the word 'Writhe'…"
"Say the word 'Search'…"
"Say the word 'Clef'…"
"Say the word 'Numb'…"
"Say the word 'Guise'…"

Driving. The late autumn sun low in the sky, I approach the traffic signal that faithfully announces "you are almost home." The car slows, rolls to a stop in a long line of others. As I stare absently at the red light, a rattling starts, a familiar pattern, muffled by the loud ruminations that always follow a rough day at work. The right side of my peripheral vision dims; that sound… it's coming from the same direction…

I turn to look; the passenger window filled with her gaunt face, rageful, spewing. Fierce eyes flash into mine as I realize the latch is being jostled in an effort to open the door. Before I can fully process what's happening, she hits the window forcefully with her palm and strides back to the sidewalk, ranting as she hurries purposefully in the other direction. The signal now green.

Some said the worst was avoidable; some said it was incorrigible.

Syllables began to shape-shift because the letters got their hearing confused. Several hid and stole away, pitched beyond return.

Some said, "All things are indeterminate." Some said, "There is a purpose to all things."

Background music ran over the tell.

Then soft rain vanished along with the chimes singing in the breeze.

The occupying force came in through the ears; the silent type, the worst kind of intruder, ready to put their feet up.

Every checkpoint closed; every synapse filled with sludge or jitters. Acquiescence assumed.

"Please see notification re: changed security protocols."

Apathetic resignation is key to survival. Resistance is futile. Feign attention. Look the part; play the role. Smile. Act as if you are listening; but keep out of earshot.

Whatever you do, don't be obvious. Don't look back.

I hear them calling her name.
I can't tell how far it is from here to her.

I can't tell if they are calling her name… or is it mine?
I hear her hiding.

I can't explain this place. I try and then don't. Who has the
energy. Everyone needing. Everyone trying to hang on,
hang in, hang on in.

Dark, dark inside this smothering sun, words hover at the edge
of erasure, dangling a first letter, its sound prancing off
my tongue reaching as it dissipates.

"Stam," a word visits in a dream.

I don't know how to tell you; I don't know how...
One (*she*), another (She), a gang of how many, a list of more,
us, them, we, you, I, they

> scratching behind walls
> vibrating the phone
> ringing the ears
> CPR, oxygen
> She is still here
> for how long?
> while *she* is disappearing
> for too long
> then the wrong name on the transfer slip
> threats following threat
> vibrating the phone
> ringing the ears
> a cop in the voicemail
> after a text
> since when do cops text?

just this side of the law
I should have known
stipulated facts
loopholes of fraud
mutating and replicating
swarming with swarms
greasing paths through the cupboards
snapping the trap
meanwhile what is *she* to do?
I should have known
she can't not go there
no visitors
no exceptions
14 days
out of an abundance of caution
essential workers only
essentially short staffed
frauds accusing fraud
ringing the ears
26 days
She is still there
and *she* wants out
absent of time
absent of touch
essential protocols apply
essential addendums
essential detentions
she wants to find a way back
and She comes to, yet again

essentially changed
I should have known
47 days
the wrong medicine in the IV
morphine under the tongue
She doesn't have the energy
She needs more than we can get
and for all *she* can't get
she needs more than we can give
out of an abundance of caution
take what you can
look who profits from disruption
look who profits from desperation
73 days
essentially betrayed
no one picking up the other end of the line
She doesn't remember
she won't say
is there anyone there…?
breathing… everything else is extra
she can't say
84 days
swarming with ants
tracking the rats
in threat upon threat
some still sing
My Country, 'Tis of Thee
while many still gasp
"I can't breathe"

and yes, once again
9 minutes
29 seconds
another cop, yet again…
while She needs all She has left to breathe
when *she* needs all *she* has left to leave
I should have known
129 days
over 4,000,000 acres
burning the nostrils
burning the throat
purple air replaces pepper spray
3 weeks
3 days
20% containment
threat following threats
preying on chaos
vibrating the phone
156 days
where has *she* gone?
how do you cry in a mask
no way to wipe the snot
greasing paths through the cupboards
scratching behind walls
fleshing the traps
where has *she* gone?
and how long does She have?
who can say how long
6 feet apart

out of an abundance of caution
15 minutes or more
no reason to expect
no reason
no touch
no agency
I should have known
breathing... everything else is extra
181 days
She drops the phone
can't see, can't hear
can't stay this way
She is gone and
she is not coming back
with all that's gone on
while they who will never leave
flesh the traps
pile the lies
un-flesh the traps
pile the bodies
bruising their faces
"Be there, will be Wild!"
replicating and mutating
swarming with swarms
just outside the law
essential mercenaries
essential training
essentially betraying
My Country, 'Tis of Thee

ringing the ears
at least 10,000
leaving feces
leaving bullet holes
snapping the trap
more than 140
more than 400,000
harassed hearts
how long do we have

"Say the word 'Nab'..."
"Say the word 'Trust'..."
"Say the word 'Mine'..."
"Say the word 'Yours'..."
"Say the word 'Cleave'..."

You said "it's not working."
I didn't ask if it was hurting.

You said "I can't move."
I didn't ask if you were ready to…

Couldn't speak of what you had never spoken.
Couldn't speak of what you chose never to open.

Couldn't say "Are you sure you don't want to . . . ?"

It was too soon… it was too late.

There she is, on the ringing phone. I pick up and sit quietly with her, forlorn and disoriented on the other end of the line. We are both sleep-deprived, depleted. She aches for a glimmer of reassurance despite, somehow, perhaps.

How much longer can this go on? All my careful words have abandoned me and I don't have the energy to go looking for them. Defiantly, because I love her, an unanticipated remark somersaults out my mouth across the room into the green beyond the window. She's mesmerized by its movement, stirred by the possibility of something animate. She insists I say more.

This time the words are hesitant, clumsy. I clip the last of them mid-speech, flick them off my fingers into the mute of clumped dust and stray hair under the sofa. She churns in the silence, yearning. Her disquiet grows huffy. She puffs the deflated phrases back into motion and snags me, raising her voice, "What did you mean? What *do* you mean?"

With no idea how to soothe her, a few raw utterances flounder up through my constricted throat. Red. Swollen. That even these might whet the grief we share I shape them rounder with "oh…s", "so…s" and "I don't know…s". She knows though; she wants an answer— something to pierce through what has happened, as much as anything I've said—an answer I don't have or know how to find. She demands I hand it over. The knife gleams, ready to cut both ways, slicing the hot afternoon sun, fulgurant, double-edged through my ear.

"Say the word 'Crave'…"
"Say the word 'Rub'…"
"Say the word 'Lapse'…"
"Say the word 'Pang'…"
"Say the word 'Wish'…"

I hear her calling my name.
I can't tell from which direction or from how far away.

I don't know if she wants a reckoning or a remedy.
I know she can't hold on much longer.

Driving. The radio plays. We don't talk. I'm relieved to not have to engage in conversation and the exhausting struggle to decipher what's being said through the rumble of road, the friction of background music. Still, the tinny frequencies and taut rhythm slash and grate at my nerves. I look at the console, surprised to see the name of a Bill Evans tune, a favorite I can still hum from memory, now unrecognizable. My ears have gutted the lush out of its rushing chords; minced the once lilting melody into a jangly elusive. The snare swishes, snaps, snap-snap-snap.

Some say "what's left to say?"
I hear "why did you stay away?"

Some say "you're not the only one."
I hear "why didn't you come?"

Others say "you did your best."
I hear "give it a rest."

A few say "it won't last forever."
I say "it's forever changed."

Most say "Move on!" I ask "where to?"

Waking in the one-year-later summer, memories smothered in
sun, I don't know how to begin another-day-with-me-in-it:
moist, torpid, a place where things churn and chew in the dark.
Out-there's bright-brightly shrilling in-here's moldering. I find
my phone and search for the last text message I sent you—
a photo of *Amaryllis Belladonna*: Naked Ladies.
Trumpets out of the duff, their cotton-candy perfume wafts
from the pixels, pierces the air pink—

     Spotty connection:

     "Are you crying?" I don't ask.
My ears struggle to hear your voice; is it cracking, or is it the
signal?

I should have known

Did you not know?
Did you not want to know?

No knowing

Present pixels
     should have's, wish I'ds, why didn't I's

No knowing

But I did
     not enough, not soon enough, not enough

The sun blares another-day-with-me-in-it: moist, torpid, a place
where things churn and chew in the dark… through parched
trees, the sweet briefly of wren song.

"Say the word 'Jab'…"
"Say the word 'Fool'…"
"Say the word 'Raw'…"
"Say the word 'Toll'…"
"Say the word 'Lose'…"

I hear you calling my name.
I can't tell if it comes from deep inside or far beyond my body.

I can't tell you what you want to hear; I can't tell you…
I hear you waiting.

"Say the word 'Sough'…"
"Say the word 'Wend'…"
"Say the word 'Roil'…"
"Say the word 'Hinge'…"
"Say the word 'Let' …"

2.

A Lexicon

.

How can we know what matters
until we know what doesn't?

Until what doesn't matter enough matters
more than we could know…

Fat splats spill from a soaked green tunnel of storm-bent trees. The windshield, a drum. The steering wheel, a swiveling chair. Swerve: rock, swerve: sludge, swerve: debris. Stop. Out of the car. Drag a large limb; clear the way. Pause… a watery quieting… I watch a box turtle lumber into the mayapple, green greening; eyes alert for salamanders. If only I could linger in the post-rain lush, but I need to get to work, on time. Swerve. Swivel. Swerve. Swerve.

Hurry, says the clock; Slow, say the woods. Conflicted, I navigate the shadowy obstacle course with more and more impatience, trying to forget the hidden treasures I must refuse. Cascades of rubble, swaths of mud, I thought it was a rock. Steering to straddle it between my wheels, I miscalculate. A crush under the tire. Panic. Out of the car. Cream-colored globules of intact lungs punctuate a pink welter of squashed viscera and smashed carapace. Her neck extended, her mouth gasping. I drop. Scan. Search. Try: can't find anything heavy enough. Try: can't muster enough force. Try: can't take full responsibility. Try: can't do it. Can't: weep. Try: weep. Try: can't. Reckless brute, do it! Can't. Weep, ruthless coward… weep… Back in the murderous car, it is late.

MISTAKEN

      : to assume

ASSUME

      : capability

CAPABILITY

      : to trust

TRUST

      : like a turtle crossing the road

ACUITY

: how exactly they game the system

: with the scent of a hungry Grizzly

: scry the bones

: *A hymn, a snare, and an exceeding sun.*
(Gwendolyn Brooks)

AMPLIFIED

What is the sound of urgency?

ASK

: not the signal, but the noise

ASSUME

    : it's salted

    : in an abundance of grief or greed

    : with a diffusion of responsibility

BACKGROUND

    : stuck in a smoke-filled heat dome

    : shitting in our own nest

    : growing the wealth gap

    : leveraging scapegoats

    : gunning down what can't be faced within

    : Pay No Attention to What's Behind the Curtain

BANDWIDTH

: of the bottom line

: of marked time

: of faulty peripheral vision

: of my frazzled nervous system

CAPABILITY

: O snake's jaw

: O pair of gloves

: O radiant gaze

: O cocked gun

: O vacant room

CLARITY

    : a refusal

    : as if your key no longer fits the door of your
      childhood home

    : *The breathing is gone; only the teeth are left.*
      (Toni Morrison)

CONFOUNDED

: the way my ears once were able to hear

: how I was once able to make you laugh

: being wont to lose my way, even with a map

DIRECTED

    : like wildfire smoke on the wind

    : like a rat scurrying to his nest

DISCORDANT

What is the sound of excusable?

DISCREPANCY

: *Their house isn't beautiful but its / shadows are.*
  (C.D. Wright)

: when broadcast in a murmur

: as if to care bespeaks a fool

DISGUISED

: as aid

: a friend's betrayal

: in acronyms

: the taste of futility

DISTORTED

: in both signal and noise

DISTRACTION

: the turkeys in my right ear gobbling up half your words

ECHOED

: familiar but unrecognizable

: this "b" for that "v" sound

: whenever they blame the victim

: each room swarming with ants…

: how I let her down; I let her down; let her down

FREQUENCY

: every morning un-fleshing the furred traps

: odorous of territorial disputes

: his voice pitched like a shrug

: waving dark money in the shape of an upside-down flag

ILLUSIVE

    : "our" justice

    : "your" land

    : certainly not these mushrooms breaking through
      the asphalt

IMPEDANCE

: when a word means the opposite of how it sounds

INDECIPHERABLE

: polite as fog at night

: like the mean streak in me

: this bureaucratic logic

: an excuse, withholding and beholden

: delay, deny, defend

Why I didn't listen, I will never know. The lights blinking on and off, on and off in our Tuba City hotel room. We were not welcome; why would we be. *Diné* land, Navajo Nation. The sky so vast, I escape into it. Uninvited.

On a late November afternoon, on our way back from Canyon de Chelly National Monument, we park our small truck on the side of a sparsely traveled road and walk with our cameras across the scrub toward a bloated cow carcass, one of several whose periodic appearances had puzzled us while driving. Quiet as deep as the horizon is wide; sun-scoured skeletons strewn across the field, an intact ribcage here, a pelvis there, a horse's entire jawbone. As young photographers, bred on a language of acquisition, we think nothing of gathering some of the best specimens to add to our collection from home: muskrat skulls from the marshes where we grew up, Holstein teeth from the fields of upstate New York where I worked on a dairy farm. We plunder with enthusiasm. Until. Until the sound of an eight-cylinder pickup speeding down the highway; its driver's eyes bore into us with visceral force.

Back on the road, after about twenty minutes, the engine starts to sputter. Sputter. Sputter. Stall. Not a person in sight. Dusk. Big flakes of snow. Hardly a sound. The rest of the story is long and winding and cold. In the end we got off easy. In the end I wish I could to tell you it was I who realized how to offer repair for our trespass, our theft, our fixation with possession. In the end, I can't.

RECOGNITION

    : for what remains

REMAINS

    : in the unspoken

UNSPOKEN

    : like sky

INDISCERNIBLE

What is the sound of complicity?

INDISTINCT

: "stillness" or "stone"

: "manage" or "damage"

: "fibroid" or "thyroid"

: "stock bait" or "start date"

: "earworm" or "wormhole"

: "get in the water" or "dead in the water"

: *The open suitcase—is it a coffin or a boat?*
(Lara Mimosa Montes)

LISTEN

: to their lack of reply

: to the questions you don't ask

: to the sting of a slap

LOCALIZATION

: the way I pronounce *recuerdo*

: (feeling your hand in the small of my back)

: a voice I cannot find, yet cannot run from

: seeded with space to grow

: despite, or due to, lack

: rhyming as if to recall and replace

: memory, or a future, undone

: here on this third stone from the sun

LOUD

: 1.5° C

: the broken promises of the Paris Accords

: a tongue burnt

: in hush money

: backchanneled and perfumed

: in Anthropocene extinctions

MISSED

: the signal in the noise

Foot on the brake. Foot on the gas. Brake. Gas. Brake. "Despite heavier than usual traffic, you are on the fastest route." Red taillights pulse in the distance… "There's a 10 minute slow down ahead; you are still on the fastest route." Gas. Brake. Brake. A police car's blue and red lights flash a few exits away. A siren. Another. A red blaze. Another. I turn the radio to the local news station. "…coming up on SoCal's only 24/7 Traffic Watch, updates every 10 on the 5; but first, here's Your Money Desk…"

Eight lanes at a complete stop now; another eight lanes creeping in the opposite direction, outlined by auto malls and big-box stores. A cloudless sky. Concrete guard rails… "and now for your commute, brought to you today by Arden Chevrolet: It's not a good morning on the Southbound 605 heading towards the 405. Highway patrol reports a fatal collision in the left two lanes as you approach Bellflower; paramedics have arrived but settle in for a long wait; a tow truck and debris from a tire blow-out on an Amazon delivery van are blocking your best alternative at Downey…"

How many lives have just been lost? How many lives connected to those lives are now profoundly changed? The driver in the lane to my left is head-down to his phone. The driver to my right is head-down to hers. A car nearby cranks up 50 Cent. In the rearview mirror a woman about my age drums her canary-yellow nails on the steering wheel. How oddly routine. I check the time.

AMPLIFIED

    : distraction

DISTRACTION

    : echoed

ECHOED

    : in simultaneity

SIMULTANEITY

    : of the here and gone

MISTAKEN

    : to assume

    : beyond a reasonable doubt

MODULATION

: what can and cannot be changed

: …remember how we used to laugh

: with carnival instinct

: the wind in the eucalyptus leaves toying with my
   hearing aids

MURMURING

: a memory of a four-year-old me in a chicory sweater

: watching my brother rock himself to sleep

: how many forever chemicals in a glass of water?

PHASING

What is the sound of attention?

POROUS

: a mystic

: in doubt

: not unlike a cloud

: sopped up with Large Language Models

PURPOSED

: for what's not put on the agenda

: how he jiggles his right foot the entire meeting

: sweating it out

: somewhere at the end of this trail of ants

: a voice I cannot locate

RECOGNITION

: though my throat constricts when I try to explain

: the squeal of my left hearing aid when you hug me goodbye

: there is no returning

REFRAIN

: the word "unprecedented"

: *There was once, and there was only once; once was all there was.*
(Ali Smith)

"Whatya doin?" a small voice asks from the curb as I lie under the front end of my old Corolla positioning a jack. Denimed legs visible below the passenger door. I pull myself out; "Replacing the brake pads," I answer and start cranking up the car.

C's friends run through the apartment driveway and stop to watch me remove the tire, chatty, before they dash off to join a group of boys who call from the small park across the street. C stays, questioning and commenting on my progress. "Yeah," he says crouched next to me when I show him the worn pads, "SPENNNT!" And then after a brief pause, "They killed M."

I stop examining the rotor and look at C looking at his feet. "M was my best friend," he continues, "I miss him… He got it when those guys drove through last week… I miss him; he was my best friend…" The freeway hums; the song of the ice cream truck loops again. "… oh well, I won't see 'em anymore …" I put down my wrench, "I'm sorry, C. That's messed up; I am so sorry." No other words show up to help. My thumb rubs at a greasy knuckle; we both stare at the ground a while. Eventually, C says, "Eve, I've got a question," his face eager again, "do you still believe in the Easter Bunny?" I watch his eyes squint, his mouth twist, "cause I'm not sure anymore; I'm startin' to think like it's not really."

LISTEN

: to the porous

POROUS

: in all uncertainty

UNCERTAINTY

: ask a child

REITERATION

: distinct from repetition

: a bump stock for a machine gun

: or how he drops his voice on the last word of every sentence

: as if burying a sound already lost

: there in our would-be mutuals…

: …did you try rebooting your phone?

REMAINS

: as the signal, noise

RESIGNED

: when my tinnitus randomly shifts higher in pitch

: to the mantic and eidetic

: amid the overwhelming scent of air "freshener" in the dentist office

: I pick at a scab of old laughter

RESONANCE

     : in a recent voicemail from a now-dead friend

     : my heart pounding in my ears

     : the impulse to look back

     : but the gods say *"Don't look back!"*

     : for how it nears

     : the way it ends

SCATTERED

: in my mother's ashes

: some sort of daughter

: with an unreliable sense of direction

SIMULTANEITY

: *Look, we're right back where we are!*
(Darlene Berens)

STARTLED

: O sliver of bone

: O cracked tooth

: O heart's auricle

: O confounded refrain

: O never mind...

STATIC

    : of the unexpected

    : sparked by your impatience with me

    : buzzing along the freeway

    : of convenience culture

TRANSLATE

: for those who have never lived without smartphones

: far from our personalized silos of on-demand

: the leftovers of disposable facts

: the tight curl of the tomato plant's leaves

: *A state of holding one's / breath forever but not dying.*
(Victoria Chang)

TRANSMIT

What is the sound of indifference?

TRUST

: can you?

: with so little water to cross the desert

: a child's unrelenting stare

UNABLE

    : to feign

    : imposed borders

    : in the teeth of famine

    : in the neck of time

UNCERTAINTY

: … *"I soon felt" / "that I" "was being followed" "I turned" "to look behind—" "a figure / vanished" "whom I just glimpsed," "a woman" "darkly robed" / "A minute later" "I saw her" "ahead of me," "where the path turned"* …
(Alice Notley)

UNFILTERED

    : like another pop-up window

    : this tightness in my chest

    : when the little white dog shivers

UNRELIABLY

: like an addict

: there on the other side of the screen

: so mirrored

UNSPOKEN

: an omen disregarded

: itching like eczema

: in the faded handwriting on a postcard sent years
before your death

: the improbable at first blush

UNSTABLE

: as is alpha in the pecking order

: on borrowed time

: at the bluff's edge

: yearning

: to hear your voice calling my name

VIBRATION

What is the sound of estrangement?

Too warm for this early in spring. Mid-day sun. Car windows rolled down for the barest of breezes, I stop at a red light. Out of the corner of my right eye, I notice a fluttering at the very edge of the passenger window, incongruent with the meager movement of air. I lean forward and tilt sideways to get a better view. Flutter, wave, wag, flutter. In the tree shaded corner of the sidewalk, atop a thigh-high cinder block wall, what appears to be a large, partially-filled, plastic trash bag flaps back and forth lackadaisically.

I turn to check the signal but immediately my peripheral vision stirs again. Flop, flap. It can't be. I crane my neck. A body balances precariously on its side atop the slim ledge of the wall: head covered in a black hoodie, torso tightly wrapped in long-sleeves, a hint of flesh at the wrist. A palm appears, waves toward the street, sways, and settles. The whole body minutely adjusts for its narrow berth. A few seconds later the hand rises up, wagging an index finger as it ascends. The finger starts to circle. It's clear I am not the intended recipient of these gesticulations but I eavesdrop anyway; an entire arm now reaching skywards, swirling with increasing speed... The car behind me honks.

TRANSLATE

    : the discrepancy

DISCREPANCY

    : in the distortion

DISTORTION

    : of what is missed

MISSED

    : in the wave of a hand like a flag

Notes

Cover Image: Margaret Watts Hughes, "Impression Figure" circa 1885-1904. Watts Hughes was a Welsh vocalist and philanthropist who invented the Eidophone—from the Greek *eidō* ("to see") and *phōnē* ("voice, sound")—which directly recorded her voice into pigment on glass. She was the first woman to present a scientific instrument of her own invention at the Royal Society of London. For more information about her amazing images and how she incorporated them into her philanthropy, please see online articles in *The Public Domain Review* and *The Marginalian*.

Epigraph: Joyelle McSweeney, from "Rat Mask," *Toxicon and Arachne* (Nightboat Books, 2020)

p. 38: Gwendolyn Brooks, from "Boy Breaking Glass," *Blacks* (Third World Press, 1991)

p. 45: Toni Morrison, from *Beloved* (Alfred A. Knopf, 1987)

p. 49: C.D. Wright, from "Treatment," *Steal Away: Selected and New Poems* (Copper Canyon Press, 2002)

p. 61: Lara Mimosa Montes, from *Thresholes* (Coffee House Press, 2020)

p. 75: Ali Smith, from *There But For The* (Pantheon, 2011)

p. 83: Darlene Berens, as quoted by Stephen Berens in a personal conversation

p. 86: Victoria Chang, from "Civility," *Obit* (Copper Canyon
         Press, 2020)

p. 90: Alice Notley, from *The Descent of Alette* (Penguin, 1996)

Acknowledgments

There are many who encouraged and supported the making of this book—I am particularly indebted to Colleen Hennessey, Adele Horne, and Susana Hennessey Lavery, who provided me refuge, sustenance, and camaraderie in the magic of Pudding Flats. To Mark Harris, Hilja Keading, John Levy and Mady Schutzman, each for their particular sensibility in providing feedback on early drafts. To Mark Harris for his trust, patience, and care with the creative process, and also for the gorgeous cover design. To the countless winged creatures who have offered song enough for even the bleakest of days. And to Kazunori Okada for all the ways he has expanded my dynamic range of being-with.

About the Author

Eve Luckring is a writer and visual artist living in Los Angeles on the unceded lands of Tovaangar. Her work questions the assumptions, and experiments with the boundaries, defining place, body, and habit. She is the author of *The Tender Between*, also published by Ornithopter Press.

www.ingramcontent.com/pod-product-compliance
Lightning Source LLC
Chambersburg PA
CBHW022156080426

42734CB00006B/451